Welcome Home, Forever Child

A Celebration of Children Adopted as Toddlers, Preschoolers, and Beyond

Written and Illustrated by
Christine Mitchell

AuthorHouse™
1663 Liberty Drive, Suite 200
Bloomington, IN 47403
www.authorhouse.com
Phone: 1-800-839-8640

AuthorHouse™ UK Ltd.
500 Avebury Boulevard
Central Milton Keynes, MK9 2BE
www.authorhouse.co.uk
Phone: 08001974150

First published by AuthorHouse 12/19/2006

ISBN: 978-1-4259-6304-0 (sc)

Library of Congress Control Number: 2006910349

Printed in the United States of America
Bloomington, Indiana

This book is printed on acid-free paper.

Bloomington, IN      Milton Keynes, UK

For my two favorite girls in the world,
and for all the waiting children

A special thank you to all those who offered
feedback and suggestions on this book

We wished so long for a child like you,

and then at last our dreams came true.

It seems that in His way God knew,

He'd found the perfect home for you.

You were past diapers, bottles, and cribs;

you would need no more booties or bibs.

Though we weren't there for your first word,

we're grateful that our prayers were heard.

We didn't watch you learn to crawl,

or give you your first bouncy ball.

We didn't share your first big grin,

or see your baby teeth come in.

Although we've missed some things, it's true,

we have a lifetime now with you.

So much to learn, so much to do;

we will share many firsts with you…

Your first time riding on a horse,

your first time camping out, of course.

Your first swim across the pool,

and your first day of middle school.

We'll rock you in the rocking chair,

and you can hug your teddy bear.

We'll count our blessings every day,

so thankful that you're here to stay.

We'll do our best to calm your fears,

and we'll be there to dry your tears.

We'll read you bedtime stories each night;

you'll see that it will be all right.

We'll take you out to trick-or-treat,

and meet the children on our street.

We're just as proud as we can be,

to have you in our family.

We'll count to twenty as you hide,

and cheer at all your games with pride.

Broken toy or game? We'll fix it.

Booboo on your knee? We'll kiss it.

We'll light the candles on your cake,

and we'll save all the crafts you make.

We'll take you to explore the zoo,

and when you're sick we'll comfort you.

We'll watch you jump and splash in puddles,

and give you lots of hugs and cuddles.

We'll help you build a castle of sand,

and when you're scared we'll hold your hand.

We'll be there for every birthday,

and for your graduation day.

And though it seems so far away,

we'll be there for your wedding day.

We'll mark your growth chart on the wall,

amazed that you have grown so tall.

Precious child, you have blessed us so,

and we love you more than you can know.

Home at last, we hope you'll see,

you've found your *Forever Family*.

Sometimes quiet, sometimes wild;

we're glad you're our *Forever Child*.

Made in the USA
San Bernardino, CA
28 February 2016